The RISE of the CITIES

1820–1920

The RISE *of* *the* CITIES

1820–1920

Christopher Collier
James Lincoln Collier

BENCHMARK BOOKS

MARSHALL CAVENDISH
NEW YORK

ACKNOWLEDGEMENT: The authors wish to thank Michael H. Ebner, A.B. Dick Professor of History and Department Chair, Lake Forest College, for his careful reading of the text of this volume of The Drama of American History and his thoughtful and useful comments. The work has been much improved by Professor Ebner's notes. The authors are greatly in his debt, but, of course, assume full responsibility for the substance of the work, including any errors that may appear.

Benchmark Books
Marshall Cavendish Corporation
99 White Plains Road
Tarrytown, NY 10591

Library of Congress Cataloging-in-Publication Data

Collier, Christopher, date
The rise of the cities / by Christopher Collier, James Lincoln Collier.
p. cm.   — (the drama of American history)
Includes bibliographical references and index.
ISBN 0-7614-1051-1
1. Cities and towns—United States—History. 2. Urbanization—United States—History.
3. City and town life—Unites States—History. I. Collier, James Lincoln, date. II. Title.
III. Series: Collier, Christopher, date Drama of American history

HT123.C58   2000   307.76'0
973—dc21 99-38409   CIP

Printed in the United States of America
1 3 5 6 4 2

CONTENTS

Over many years of both teaching and writing for students at all levels, from grammar school to graduate school, it has been borne in on us that many, if not most, American history textbooks suffer from trying to include everything of any moment in the history of the nation. Students become lost in a swamp of factual information, and as a consequence lose track of how those facts fit together and why they are significant and relevant to the world today.

In this series, our effort has been to strip the vast amount of available detail down to a central core. Our aim is to draw in bold strokes, providing enough information, but no more than is necessary, to bring out the basic themes of the American story, and what they mean to us now. We believe that it is surely more important for students to grasp the underlying concepts and ideas that emerge from the movement of history, than to memorize an array of facts and figures.

The difference between this series and many standard texts lies in what has been left out. We are convinced that students will better remember the important themes if they are not buried under a heap of names, dates, and places.

In this sense, our primary goal is what might be called citizenship education. We think it is critically important for America as a nation and Americans as individuals to understand the origins and workings of the public institutions that are central to American society. We have asked ourselves again and again what is most important for citizens of our democracy to know so they can most effectively make the system work for them and the nation. For this reason, we have focused on political and institutional history, leaving social and cultural history less well developed.

This series is divided into volumes that move chronologically through the American story. Each is built around a single topic, such as the Pilgrims, the Constitutional Convention, or immigration. Each volume has been written so that it can stand alone, for students who wish to research a given topic. As a consequence, in many cases material from previous volumes is repeated, usually in abbreviated form, to set the topic in its historical context. That is to say, students of the Constitutional Convention must be given some idea of relations with England, and why the Revolution was fought, even though the material was covered in detail in a previous volume. Readers should find that each volume tells an entire story that can be read with or without reference to other volumes.

Despite our belief that it is of the first importance to outline sharply basic concepts and generalizations, we have not neglected the great dramas of American history. The stories that will hold the attention of students are here, and we believe they will help the concepts they illustrate to stick in their minds. We think, for example, that knowing of Abraham Baldwin's brave and dramatic decision to vote with the small states at the Constitutional Convention will bring alive the Connecticut Compromise, out of which grew the American Senate.

Each of these volumes has been read by esteemed specialists in its particular topic; we have benefited from their comments.

CHAPTER I

The First
American Cities

It is impossible to imagine modern life without cities. It is true that today the majority of Americans live outside of cities in the suburbs, small towns, or the countryside. Yet by far the majority of Americans live in what are called "metropolitan areas"—that is, a city and the suburbs that surround it. We may live in suburbs, but our lives are focused on cities. They are where the majority of Americans work, where the sports and entertainment so important to us are produced, where the financial systems are controlled, where our medical centers and our museums, concert halls, and other cultural institutions are located. For most Americans, life is centered on cities.

Given how important cities are to us today, it is surprising how recently they came among human societies. A few very small cities—hardly more than small towns—sprang up perhaps ten thousand years ago, but there were very few of them in the whole world. Only slowly did cities grow in number and size. As recently as two hundred years ago the vast majority of human beings around the world—over 90 percent—

Big cities, with their towering office buildings, their theaters and restaurants and clubs, their sports arenas and financial and news-gathering centers, are at the heart of American life. This picture of Chicago at night suggests the glamour and power we associate with cities.

lived in villages, on farms, or wandered as nomads through prairies and deserts.

Nonetheless, cities have always been more important to us than their numbers suggest. Kings, priests, and parliaments have usually reigned from cities. The rulers of ancient cities like Rome, Alexandria, Babylon, and Peking often dominated huge areas of land around them; and in more recent times it was people living in cities like Venice, Paris, Timbuktu, and Tenochtitián that commanded their cultures, producing the ideas and the wealth that made their societies important.

Most of the people who lived under the great Roman Empire, which lasted for a thousand years, were farmers, or even nomads. Nonetheless, this great empire was ruled from Rome during most of that span of time. This picture shows the ruins of the Roman Forum as they look today. They suggest how grand this mighty city was two thousand years ago.

The English people who first came to America lived in small villages or on farms scattered across the countryside. But very quickly towns began to arise. At first these were seaports, growing naturally at good harbors, frequently where rivers or bays connected with the Atlantic Ocean, like Boston, New York, and Philadelphia. At these places products from the inland fields and forests, like tobacco, wheat, furs, and timber, were brought for shipment to markets in Europe, the West Indies, and elsewhere. Here also ships unloaded imported goods, such as paint, window glass, and furniture, that Americans wanted to buy. Inevitably, there grew up around these harbors wharfs, warehouses, business offices, and fine houses for the merchants who owned those warehouses and the ships that came and went.

These little towns, at first quite small, attracted artisans and craftsmen who could turn the raw material coming from the countryside into finished goods: tanners and cobblers to make hides into shoes, shipbuilders to turn timber into hulls and masts, wheelwrights to shape iron and wood into wagons and carts. The towns also attracted many laboring people who laid bricks for new houses, unloaded ships, drove carts from ships to warehouses, and manned the ships that carried American products up and down the Atlantic Coast, to the Caribbean, to Europe. Inns, taverns, and rooming houses sprang up to shelter these transient populations.

As the population and the commerce of America grew, so did these port communities, and by 1700 there were several places that could be called cities, at least in terms of that time. The most important of these were Boston, with seven thousand people; New York and Philadelphia with four thousand each; and Newport, Rhode Island, and Charleston, South Carolina, with lesser numbers. There was a limit to how large these early cities could grow. There was little public transportation; cities had to be small enough so that the inhabitants could easily walk from their homes to their jobs. Historians thus sometimes refer to them as "walking cities." Houses were two or three stories high. Streets were narrow and muddy in wet weather, dusty in dry. Shops were small; A tailor might have a room where his customers came, with a workshop behind and living quarters upstairs for himself and his family. Clustered in the center of such cities were a few grand buildings used by the government, like Philadelphia's famous building, today known as Independence Hall. Also within walking distances were churches, the mansions of the rich, taverns, stables, and craftsmen and shopkeepers living in small houses circling around the town center. On the outskirts in shanties and shacks

Charleston, like most of the first American cities, developed around a harbor on the Atlantic seacoast. The two- and three-story buildings we see here are typical of the late Colonial period.

lived laborers, sailors, the outright poor, and inevitably some beggars and criminals.

You could walk across such cities in less than half an hour. Yet small as they were, they were full of bustle and movement, with wagon loads of goods crowding the streets, ships packed with crates and barrels setting off for dangerous sea voyages. The poor rubbed elbows with the rich in the streets. Carts and wagons splashed mud on passersby.

In these cities an ambitious young man could rise in the world, apprenticing himself to a goldsmith or cartwright, and in due course becoming a master craftsman himself. Then, as a prosperous merchant dealing in goods, he would become an attractive prospective husband for the daughters of other rising men. By the middle of the 1700s there existed in these cities a wealthy elite of merchants, lawyers, shipowners—with their wives and children—who controlled things. They not only ran the main businesses but also became mayors, judges, and city councilors.

These cities, too, were home to newspapers, a few small libraries, small but growing universities like Harvard, near Boston, Yale in New Haven, and William and Mary in Williamsburg. Inevitably, the cities were places where ideas were discussed and developed. In the mid-1700s people in cities were beginning to talk about the rights and duties of Americans in respect to the mother country, England. It was in cities like Boston and Philadelphia that people began to insist that Americans should not be dominated by the rulers in London, but ought to have certain freedoms.

The American Revolution was fomented mainly in cities, for it was in cities that people could easily gather to hear the speeches and debates on the question of breaking away from England. In Boston, citizens, urged on by fiery speeches, served up the famous Boston Tea Party; and it was Bostonians who organized the battles at Concord and Lexington, which triggered the American Revolution. (Readers interested in the details of these events can find them in the volume in this series called *The American Revolution 1763–1783*).

After the war, it was also mainly people from cities who provided the ideas and the leadership for an independent United States; and it was mainly city people who wrote the American Constitution in Philadelphia in 1787. To be sure, some of the American leaders of the day, like George Washington, James Madison, and Thomas Jefferson, were Southerners living on large plantations in the countryside. But they were the exception, and in any event, they congregated in cities like Williamsburg and Charleston for political purposes. One historian has written, "Though less than 5 percent of the population was urban, it was in cities that the coincidence of people, events, ideas, and leadership forged both a sense of American nationalism and a revolution." We need to keep this idea firmly in mind: Things can happen where people are clustered together that rarely occur where people are spread out over the land.

The wealth of these early American cities was not produced by factories churning out goods, but by "commerce," that is, buying, selling, and shipping the raw materials produced so abundantly in the Americas, and bringing in manufactured goods from Europe, especially England and France—chinaware, carpets, silver and pewter tableware, textiles, paint— that the rough new country was so in need of. American artisans like cobblers, tailors, and cabinetmakers did make a lot of goods; but the bulk of such items came from abroad, and the way to wealth was in buying and selling.

The first American cities, thus, developed as ports and thrived on commerce. But by the early 1800s another type of city was growing up in the "hinterlands," the inland areas away from the coast. As we shall see in more detail later, during these years the creation of machines to do what had always been done by hand was growing at an explosive rate. This "industrial revolution" had begun in England in the 1700s, and was spreading across Europe, the Americas, and elsewhere. (Readers interested in the development of industry in America can consult the volume in this series called *The Rise of Industry 1860–1900*.)

Machines need power; and in the early 1800s the major source of power was swiftly running water, which could be used to turn huge millwheels, often as much as twenty feet high. The United States was rich in streams and creeks. While it is true that many early cities were built on major rivers, slower-moving currents were not, for a variety of reasons, suitable for water mills. These rivers were too wide to build dams across and usually lacked firm rocky banks to anchor the dams. The new water-powered factories had mostly to be built in the countryside where there was a swift stream, narrow but large enough so that it would not dry up in the summer.

There were, thus, practical reasons for building factories in the country. But there were philosophical reasons for it, too. In England, where the industrial revolution had first taken hold, industry had mainly grown in cities. These cities filled up with underpaid workers coming in from the countryside in search of jobs. Very soon there appeared in such cities disease-ridden, crime-haunted slums, where impoverished working people lived desperate lives in squalid conditions.

Many Americans had visited England, and they knew about these industrial slums. A lot of them concluded that cities were natural breeding grounds for crime, disease, alcoholism. It seemed to them that country people were not merely healthier but more virtuous than city people. Many Americans, thus, did not want to see cities, with their slums, arise in America. The philosopher-president Thomas Jefferson for one, firmly believed that Americans ought to stay on their farms and let the decadent Europeans produce the manufactured goods in their corrupt cities.

There were, thus, both practical and philosophical reasons for building factories in the country. There was only one problem: Factories needed a lot of workers, and in the country, people were scattered far and wide, most of them living too far from the factory to walk there every day.

One answer was to build dwellings for workers around the factory. An early type of mill town much studied by historians was created for his textile mills by Samuel Slater in the 1790s in Pawtucket, Rhode Island, and later around what is now Webster, Massachusetts. Slater built houses for the families of his workers, along with churches, shops, and even farms where food for his workers was grown. Frequently he would sign on whole families to work in his mills—children, with their small hands, were thought to be especially good at tying the little knots textile making required. Industrialists like Slater believed they were performing a social duty by providing work for young people; they also thought they had an obligation to look after their workers' morals. Slater started one of the earliest Sunday schools in the United States, where his young workers learned about the Bible.

An early nineteenth-century mill town shows the houses of the workers clustered around the mill, which is located on the stream that turned the waterwheel. This is a factory making gun parts established by Eli Whitney, which was a forerunner of the modern factory built around an assembly line.

The most famous of their experiments with mill towns took place in Massachusetts at a site named Lowell, where textile factories had been built in 1820 by a group of investors initially headed by Francis Cabot Lowell. In order to attract farm women to work in these factories, the owners built dormitories for them. These young women, many of them still in their mid-teens, were fed and housed by the mill owners. In addition, their lives were carefully supervised to make sure that they did not fall into the sin and error it was believed factory towns tended to produce.

At the same time that these industrial cities were being built along streams, mainly in the Northeast, a third type of city was developing even farther away from the port cities of the Atlantic Coast. As far back as the 1500s, French, Spanish, and English explorers, traveling mainly on the rivers and lakes of the American interior, had established trading posts and forts for various purposes. By the early 1800s some of these posts had attracted people coming into the wilderness to trap furs, explore for metal ores, take up farmland, or simply to speculate in land. A number of these posts had grown into little settlements.

A typical case was St. Louis, Missouri. Founded by the French as a supply point on the Mississippi River, which they controlled, it had grown over time. By 1775 it had a population of about one thousand—traders, riverboat men, soldiers, shippers, trappers, frontiersmen. And by 1821 it was a town of five thousand people, and growing into a city.

Other cities, mostly located on great rivers or lakes, grew in much the same way. Pittsburgh started as a fort and grew through shipping goods down the Ohio and Mississippi Rivers to the important port city of New Orleans, and by supplying goods to the settlers carving farms out of the forests in the wild lands around the old fort. Cincinnati underwent a similar process, growing tenfold between 1810 and 1830. Many other places grew as fast. At first these young cities brought in almost all their manufactured goods from the cities of the East; but in time they too began to produce their own goods.

As it became clear that a lot of money was being made in these small western cities, enterprising promoters began planning brand-new cities of their own. The idea was to buy a piece of forestland at a promising location, draw up a map showing streets, highways, and often, churches, banks, and schoolhouses where in fact there was as yet nothing but woods, and persuade other people to buy building lots. Hundreds of such towns were created out of air. Most of them came to very little. Some

St. Louis started as an outpost for French traders and trappers. Its location on the Mississippi made it a natural point for commerce, and by the early 1800s it was growing into a real city, whose citizens took pride in its fine buildings and pleasant houses.

never existed beyond the gaudy maps their promoters published. Others attracted buyers and prospered for awhile, and then stagnated, remaining small towns. But a few of these fabricated cities, among them Lexington, Kentucky, managed to survive.

The seeds for the American cities to come were, thus, planted in dif-

Chicago started as a fort and trading post. Here Indians, in the early nineteenth century, arrive with goods to trade. Chicago's growth was extremely swift: Within fifty years this little clutch of log buildings had become a booming city.

ferent soils, some growing around natural harbors, some pulled together to support mills and factories, some growing naturally from small wilderness settlements, some spun out of the heads of optimistic promoters. But however and wherever planted, by the early 1800s there existed in the United States several dozen towns and small cities that were destined to grow into great cities around which so much of American life is built today.

CITIES OF THE WESTERN WORLD

The rapid growth of cities was occurring in many places in the world. Cities like London, Paris, and Berlin were growing rapidly. But the American cities were growing at a much faster rate than many elsewhere. By 1760, fifteen years before the outbreak of the American Revolution, Philadelphia was second only to London, England in all of the British Empire. Between 1875 and 1900 Chicago was the world's fastest-growing city, larger than Berlin in Germany in 1910 and nearly as large as Paris.

CHAPTER II

The Explosion
of the Cities

By 1820, then, there existed perhaps two dozen places that had the potential to grow into cities, or were already doing just that. But what happened next was beyond the imagining of most Americans of that time, for the way cities exploded over the next forty years has rarely been seen anywhere at any time. In 1820 about 7 percent of Americans lived in cities—and one-third of those lived in just two places—New York and Philadelphia. In that year there were only twelve cities in America with populations over 10,000 and only two over 100,000; by 1860 there were 101 cities with populations above 10,000; eight over 100,000; and one—New York—with a population of more than a million. In 1820 nearly everybody lived on farms or in villages. By 1860, 20 percent of Americans lived in cities and towns. At the time that the Constitution was written in 1787 there were only about three million people in the entire country; by 1860 there were that many living in cities alone. By 1900 one-third of all Americans lived in cities. By 1920, the year our story ends, over half of all Americans lived in urban places. In 2000 about half of the U.S. population lived in cities and another quarter lived in the densely populated immediate suburbs.

America, thus, was rapidly transforming itself from a nation of farmers to one of city dwellers working in shops, mills, factories. As noted above, the movement climaxed in 1920; but already, by 1860, the cities had come to dominate the nation. In cities lay the offices from which was

13 LARGEST CITIES IN 1820 AND 1920			
1820		**1920**	
1. New York	123,700	1. New York	5,620,000
2. Philadelphia	112,800	2. Chicago	2,701,705
3. Baltimore	62,700	3. Philadelphia	1,823,779
4. Boston	43,300	4. Detroit	993,678
5. New Orleans	27,200	5. Cleveland	796,841
6. Charleston	24,800	6. St. Louis	772,897
7. Washington	13,200	7. Boston	748,060
8. Salem	12,700	8. Baltimore	733,826
9. Albany	12,600	9. Pittsburgh	588,343
10. Richmond	12,100	10. Los Angeles	576,673
11. Providence	11,800	11. Buffalo	506,775
12. Cincinnati	9,600	12. San Fancisco	506,676
13. Norfolk	8,500	13. Milwaukee	457,147

managed the burgeoning industrial machine, eventually to be the greatest in the world. From then, by 1860 there radiated outward canals, railroad tracks, and telegraph cables that wove the cities together in a great manufacturing network. By the end of the nineteenth century, cities were setting the tone, the style, for the United States.

What caused cities to explode this way? Why did it happen with such

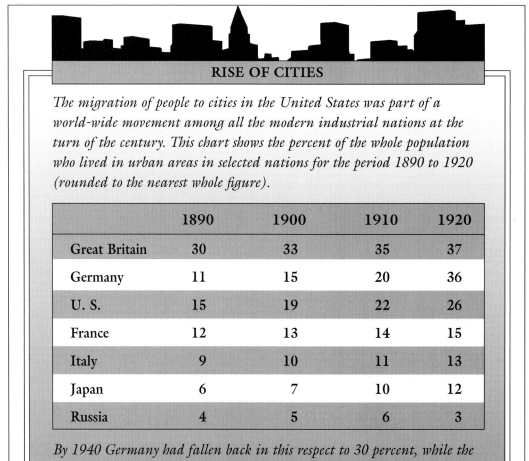

RISE OF CITIES

The migration of people to cities in the United States was part of a world-wide movement among all the modern industrial nations at the turn of the century. This chart shows the percent of the whole population who lived in urban areas in selected nations for the period 1890 to 1920 (rounded to the nearest whole figure).

	1890	1900	1910	1920
Great Britain	30	33	35	37
Germany	11	15	20	36
U. S.	15	19	22	26
France	12	13	14	15
Italy	9	10	11	13
Japan	6	7	10	12
Russia	4	5	6	3

By 1940 Germany had fallen back in this respect to 30 percent, while the United States' urban population had increased to 33 percent.

speed, so that a child growing up in the 1830s found herself living in a vastly different nation as she was rearing her own children?

The key was *industrialization*—the replacement of hand labor by machines, fueled by astonishing new inventions and technical advances, like the spinning jenny, which replaced the old hand spinning wheel, and the mechanical reaper, which could cut wheat or hay far faster than a

This advertisement from about 1850 for the new farm machinery shows at right four men reaping wheat using the old cradle sythe, while in the picture below one man is doing the same work with a mechanical reaper.

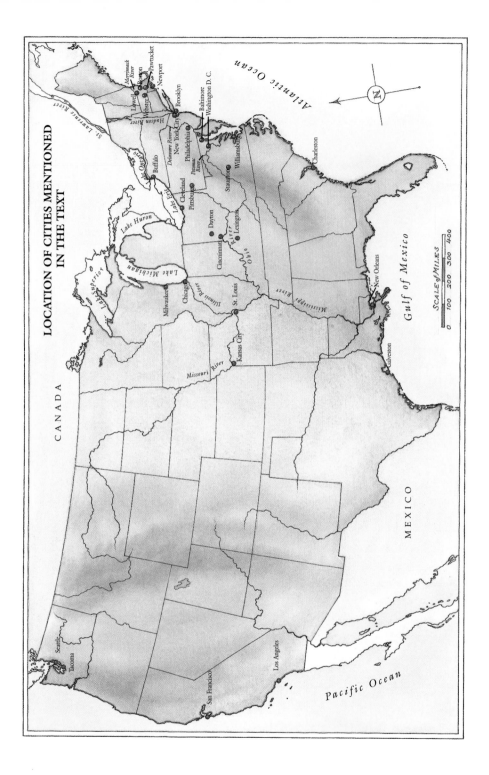

LOCATION OF CITIES MENTIONED IN THE TEXT

Merrimack River
Lowell
Pawtucket
Nashua
Webster
Newport
Brooklyn
Hudson River
New York City
Baltimore
Washington D.C.
Buffalo
Delaware River
Philadelphia
Potomac River
Lake Ontario
Charleston
Lake Erie
Cleveland
Staunton
Pittsburgh
Williamsburg
Lake Huron
Dayton
Lexington
Cincinnati
Ohio River
Lake Michigan
Wabash River
Illinois River
St. Louis
New Orleans
Milwaukee
Chicago
Gulf of Mexico
Lake Superior
Kansas City
Missouri River
Mississippi River
Galveston
St. Lawrence River
Atlantic Ocean
CANADA
MEXICO
Seattle
Tacoma
Los Angeles
San Francisco
Pacific Ocean

SCALE of MILES
0 100 200 300 400

man could using a scythe. People who had grown up doing the farm labor that had been at the heart of human life for thousands of years now found themselves working in factories and living amid crowds, instead of under open skies in little villages or isolated farms tucked away in the countryside. The industrial revolution was just that, for in a few short decades it changed human life more radically than anything since people had first begun to farm ten thousand years earlier.

When we think of the industrial revolution we usually see factories filled with clattering machines. In fact, perhaps just as important to the rise of the cities was the invention of machines for speeding up the agricultural work that had been done by hand. Though the first half of the 1800s new farm machines tumbled out one after another: mechanical reapers, mechanical cream separators, mechanical hay balers, binders, and many more. These machines drastically speeded up farming jobs. To give just one example, the early mechanical reaper, pulled by a horse, could do the work of four or five men using the old hand scythe with cradles. This meant, of course, that far fewer people could produce much more. For instance, in 1820 it took fifty to sixty man-hours to produce twenty bushels of wheat; by 1930 it took only about three hours. Although the number of people working on farms increased till about 1916, city dwellers increased much, much faster. In 1820 the majority of Americans were engaged in growing and processing food; by the year 2000, 2 percent of the population was producing enough food for everybody, with a lot left over for export.

The great surplus of foodstuffs meant that in the decades after the Civil War prices for farm produce fell—especially in relation to the prices farmers had to pay for the new machinery. Many were forced out of farming; many more decided that all that hard work was just not worth the tiny income it produced. If not the farmers, their sons and daughters fled to the rapidly growing—and exciting—cities.

But there was more to the tug of the cities than just more rewarding work. To a teenager on a farm doing the same routine work over and over, year after year, the cities seemed mighty glamorous. There were plays and concerts in the cities, shops full of goods, lively crowds to mingle with. We take such things for granted today, but in the nineteenth century, life on American farms was often boring. Your social life was limited to your family and a few neighbors and there was very little entertainment. For many young people the most exciting part of the week was church on Sunday. Furthermore, the work was hard: Wood had to be sawed even if there was a freezing rain, hay cut and raked in the baking heat of July. Women

Country people, who knew cities from only brief visits, or simply from pictures and stories, believed they were glamorous places, filled with fun and excitement. Pictures like this one of Harry Hill's famous saloon in New York in the post-Civil War period encouraged this opinion. Note the women smoking, considered very sinful at the time.

and girls spent endless hours, especially in winter, sitting day after day in cold farmhouses turning their spinning wheels or cranking butter churns, often with no company but the cat. By contrast the cities seemed filled with wonders. So they came, pulled by the glamour, and driven by the tedium, loneliness, and hard physical toil of farm life.

The cities, however, could not have exploded as they did without yet another element in the technological advances of the time—the creation of a great transportation network. In Europe, which had been settled for centuries, there existed well-traveled rivers, canal systems, familiar sea routes along the coasts, even networks of roads, some of them dating back almost two thousand years to Roman times. Travel from one European city to the next was not as easy as it is today, but it was practical: Trade between Antwerp and Venice, for instance, and London and Paris, had been going on for centuries.

No such transportation system existed in the

Canal systems had existed for centuries in Europe. This picture shows some of the canals of Venice, already being used as the city's main system of transportation of goods by medieval times.

United States. The problems of moving people and goods from one place to another over land were formidable. The great Appalachian Mountain chain divided people on the Atlantic coastal plains from people living in the rich lands of what we now call the Midwest. Even on the coastal plain travel by land was difficult: Roads were few, exceedingly rough, often cut by unbridged streams and rivers that had to be forded. In 1800 a trip overland from New York to Boston, about 200 miles, could take four days for a person on horseback; moving a wagon load of goods took even longer.

By far the easiest way to move anything was by water. Most people and goods, therefore, traveled along rivers, across lakes, or by sea along the coasts. But natural bodies of water did not always run where people wanted to go. A farmer in the hinterlands who did not live near a good-sized creek or river would have to carry his sacks of wheat or barrels of apples a long way by wagon to get them to market. Thus, even before the United States was formed people had been thinking of building canals to link towns and cities with each other and with the countryside. But at a time when there were no bulldozers and backhoes, canals had to be dug by hand with picks and shovels. By 1815 few canals had been dug in the United States.

Many people, however, had seen that a canal across New York State, running from Lake Erie to the Hudson River, would in one stroke tie the Eastern seacoast to the Great Lakes, and through them to the Ohio-Mississippi River system, linking much of the country by water. It would be a formidable task; but in 1817 Governor DeWitt Clinton of New York decided to give the Erie Canal state financing. Digging took years, but in 1825 it was complete—363.3 miles of canal. The opening of the Erie Canal, according to one historian, was the single most important event in the history of American transportation. Not only could people and goods move faster by the new water network but they could move more cheaply too. In 1817, the year the canal was started, it cost twenty cents

The digging of the Erie Canal was a critically important event in American history, for it not only opened a water route from the Atlantic to the American Midwest but showed that canals were practical ways of moving people and goods through the nation.

to carry a ton of freight a mile; by the 1850s the price, via the Erie Canal, was down to less than a penny per ton-mile. In 1836, 58,000 tons of goods traveled along the famous canal; fourteen years later tonnage had increased more than a hundred times, to 1.8 million tons. When the canal was begun, it took about ten days to travel from New York City to Buffalo; in 1830 you could make it in four days via the Erie Canal. The creation of this great water route from the Atlantic Ocean into the Great Lakes region was an important factor in spurring the rapid growth of cities like Cleveland, Detroit, Chicago, and Milwaukee.

The success of the Erie Canal spurred a huge boom in canal building. Everywhere, businessmen and urban leaders wanted to connect their cities to other cities and outlying farming areas to make sure that trade came their way. Canals were dug everywhere. Many of them were unprofitable and failed. Even so, by 1860 America was tied together by a network of canals.

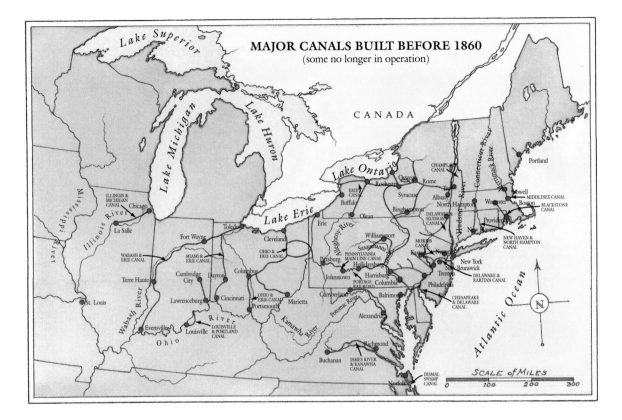

MAJOR CANALS BUILT BEFORE 1860
(some no longer in operation)

But as the canals were spreading their fingers across the countryside, an even better transportation system was being constructed. Practical steam engines had been developed in England in the 1700s, and in 1825 a railroad line was established there. American promoters were quick to see the advantages of railroads, and by 1827 a few short freight lines were under construction. The first major line, the Baltimore and Ohio, began construction in 1828 and thereafter railroads spread rapidly. Through the 1830s railroads were built throughout the Northeast, and even in the still sparsely settled Midwest. By 1860, that four-day trip from New York to Buffalo could be done in a single day.

As had been the case with the canals, towns and cities soon felt that they had to have railroad lines running into them from other cities and the countryside, so they would not be cut off from the flow of trade. Businessmen wanted produce, like wheat, iron ore, and timber, to flow into

This picture of Old Ironsides, the famous Baldwin company's first locomotive, built in 1831, shows how primitive the first railroad trains were. The passenger car is designed like a horse-drawn carriage of the time.

their cities; and they wanted to be able to ship the products of these raw materials, like flour, iron, ingots, and lumber, to other cities, even other countries. So desperate were businessmen to make sure they got a railroad that they began subsidizing railroad companies with the cities' money—in the end, money from taxpayers.

In some cases these investments paid off, but in the majority of cases the railroad promoters were paid far too much. Sometimes the railroad lines never got built at all. When they did get built, they frequently were poorly constructed and needed much work to make them efficient. Inevitably, with so much money floating around, bribes were paid by the city fathers and state legislatures to get the railroad promoters to locate rail lines and stations in their towns. Few events in American industrialization have been so scandalous as the building of the railroad system. (The story of railroad development is told in the volume in this series called *Indians, Cowboys, and Farmers and the Battle for the Great Plains*.)

Nonetheless, by 1860 a great and still growing railroad system was in place, tying the nation together with an even swifter transportation system than the canals provided. In 1800 it took about eight days to travel from New York to Pittsburgh. By 1830, with the canals, it was down to three days; and in 1860, via railroad, it was one day.

The water system of canals, rivers, and lakes was still important—the Mississippi River system, including the Ohio, the Missouri, and smaller rivers, would remain an important part of the American transportation system nearly to the end of the 1800s. But the future lay with the railroads.

Improving the efficiency of the railroads was another technological development, the telegraph system. Skilled telegraph operators could send

By 1864, when this lithograph was made, railroad technology and design had improved substantially. In the distance behind the train can be seen a steamboat, another adaptation of the steam engine to transportation.

along the cables the "Morse code" alphabet of short and long clicks or buzzes that could be rapidly translated into words. With these new devices for virtually instantaneous communication, railroads could better coordinate railway traffic and keep to their schedules. The telegraph aided industry in many other ways. Prices could be requested, orders placed, and instructions given within minutes, instead of over days by mail.

The transportation web of water and rail by itself was an important force in the growth of the city. Farmers wanting to see what city life was all about now had easy, cheap ways of making a visit. City dwellers hearing of opportunities in new, fast-growing cities farther west could make a quick trip to investigate. And they would find in these rapidly growing cities jobs created by the flood of raw materials pouring in from the countryside they had left.

All cities did not benefit from the transportation revolution, however. Canal and railway routes tended to concentrate population in certain places and draw businesses and people away from places not served by boats and trains. Thus, some once-active towns just dried up and even disappeared.

The population of American cities was not growing solely because of people arriving on trains from the farms. Equally important was the arrival of millions of immigrants from overseas, especially Europe. The tale of immigration to America is a large one; we can only sketch in the outlines here. (Readers interested in a more complete description of nineteenth-century immigration to America will find it in the volume in this series called *A Century of Immigration 1820–1924*.)

It is a truism to say that America is a land of immigrants. The English who established the first European settlements in Jamestown and Plymouth were immigrants, and so were others who followed in the 1600s and 1700s, most of them from the British Isles. But when we use the term *immigrants* we usually think of the great mass of people who swarmed into the United States in the years between 1820 and 1920. (There has

Although Ellis Island has long been celebrated as the gateway into America for immigrants, in fact it only opened in 1892. Before that the main immigration center in New York was Castle Garden, at what is now Battery Park.

been another wave of immigrants beginning in about 1970, but that is a later story.)

Just as many American migrants to the cities were *pushed* off the land by changing conditions, and *pulled* into the cities by the jobs and glamour they thought they would find in them, so the immigrants from abroad were pushed out of their homelands by bad conditions and pulled toward the United States, rather than other places, by the opportunities they thought existed here.

In some cases these immigrants were driven out by poverty, famine, and even starvation. In other cases the turmoil of war and revolution caused them to turn their eyes away from their native lands. In yet other cases the oppressiveness of landlords and rulers was the cause.

Contributing to the pressure on people to leave Europe was a great explosion of the European population after about 1750: The population there grew from 140 million to 260 million in the century before 1850 and to 400 million in 1915, when it began to level off.

The first of this great wave of nineteenth-century European immigrants was the Irish. In the 1600s Ireland had been largely taken over by the English, and by 1800 Englishmen owned most of the land there. They forced the Irish to pay high rents and soon some 80 percent of Irish people were living in the worst sort of poverty imaginable, dependent on easily grown potatoes for the bulk of their food. Then in the 1830s and 1840s there came a series of potato blights, which ruined the crops. Tens of thousands actually died in these great famines. Millions of Irish were living on the edge of starvation. So they left Ireland.

These Irish had had enough of farm life, where they had been ground down by their landlords, and mostly chose to work in mills, especially the textile mills of New England. Thus they tended to stay in cities.

The second group to arrive in large numbers was the Germans, driven out of their native land by several factors, including changes in agriculture and the politically inspired revolutionary movements of 1830 and 1848. The Germans settled in many parts of the United States, but a great many went to the Midwest, filling up cities like St. Louis, Cincinnati, Chicago, and Milwaukee. Indeed, Milwaukee, St. Louis, and Cincinnati became known as the "German triangle." There are still many descendants of these early Ger-man immigrants living in those cities.

The Germans were more likely to try farming than the Irish. For one thing, they often came with a little money to buy cheap land still available in the Midwest. But at least half of them became city dwellers, working at trades like brewing, baking, and tailoring.

One very important effect of Irish and German immigration was that Catholicism became a major religion in American. The United States had been founded by Protestants, and while colonial Maryland was started as

Nonetheless, from 1892 to 1924, when immigration slackened, millions of new Americans poured through Ellis Island. Here a young woman is getting the required medical checkup before being admitted.

a haven for Catholics, Catholics remained unwelcome in many places. But the millions of Irish pouring in were mainly Catholics; and while a large percentage of Germans were Lutherans, another large percentage were Catholics. Very quickly Irish and German communities established Catholic churches, and that religion began to grow in importance in the United States.

Despite the numbers of Germans who settled on farms, the bulk of immigrants settled in cities, and would continue to do so. The cities, thus, were drawing on two sources for population—the American farms and European nations. Welding these diverse groups into unified communities would prove to be immensely difficult.

CHAPTER III

Technology and the City

By 1860, then, the cities that had been founded decades before had grown in the most astonishing fashion. Nonetheless, the United States was still largely a rural place: 80 percent of the population still lived on farms or in small villages. In the next fifty years that would change as America became an urban nation.

This dramatic shift in American life could not have happened without an equally dramatic burst of technological advance. Indeed, the burst of invention and technological development that came in the years after the Civil War, in America as well as elsewhere, was beyond anything that has happened before or since. Today we believe we are seeing a massive explosion of new technologies, with VCRs, car phones, computers, and a whole "virtual world" in cyberspace. But recent improvements are nothing compared with what went on in the second half of the 1800s.

The most important of the new technologies of the 1800s was steam power. The principles behind the steam engine had been known for some

The early water- and steam-powered mills depended upon an elaborate system of belts to transmit power from the source to the machines around the mill. The Wilkinson Mill, in Massachusetts, now restored, still contains machinery dating back to the days of waterpower.

time, and practical steamboats and steam locomotives had been in use for decades. But not until the 1840s was steam widely adapted to run machines. Though used much earlier on a small scale, the power of stationary steam engines was introduced on a wide scale to New England textile mills in the years after 1847, and very rapidly factories everywhere switched from waterpower to steam.

The advantages were obvious and benefited cities immensely. With waterpower, factories were always at the mercy of the weather—cold spells would freeze the mill run and ice up the wheel; droughts would reduce the mill run to a trickle. Steam engines ran regardless of the weather. Further, it was no longer necessary to locate mills on fast-moving streams, which might lie at a distance from good transportation and the homes of workers. Henceforth, factories would be built in cities where there was an abundant supply of labor, and railroad and ship transportation was right at hand.

The switch to steam also had other effects on American industry. Steam engines required millions of tons of coal, which greatly increased mining operations. The coal in turn had to be carried to the cities, which meant more miles of heavy-duty rails and railroad cars to run over them. This in turn increased the demand for high-quality steel; and the making of steel demanded more millions of tons of coal, again increasing the need for more rails, and more coal hoppers. There was a spiraling effect, ratcheting the whole system upward. Not surprisingly, the second half of the 1800s has been called the Age of Steam.

In 1864 the Bessemer converter was introduced, making it possible to produce high-quality steel cheaply. This new system alone permitted the development of steel-frame skyscrapers, steel bridges, improved railroad tracks, and much else. In the 1870s practical electric dynamos were developed, which made electrically driven machines possible. The first successful telephone call was made in 1876. Sound recording was developed in the 1880s; experiments with refrigerated railroad cars began in 1888 to revolutionize the diet of urban Americans; automobiles and the motion picture came to fruition in the 1890s. In 1903 the first airplane was flown. Think of it: In a period of about twenty years there were introduced the telephone, electric lights, movies, cars, and planes. The effect on the nation—and the world—had to be profound.

So technological developments continued to come in with a rush. Just as steam-driven transportation and industry came to dominate city growth, inventors and engineers were developing a new power source that in the twentieth century would come to dominate every phase of modern life—the electric dynamo. This is a machine that converts mechanical energy into electricity. It was developed over several decades in the second half of the nineteenth century through experiments by many scientists. The man who is best known for inventing ways to put this electricity to work is Thomas Alva Edison.

As a boy, Edison was a poor student, but an avid reader. His teachers called him "addled," and his mother took him out of school and taught him herself. He was no good at mathematics, but loved chemistry, and when he was about ten he set up a laboratory in his room at home. In his laboratory all the bottles were labeled "poison," so he got the reputation of being something of a weird genius. At sixteen, in 1863, he began work as a telegraph operator, and soon began inventing ways to improve the telegraph equipment.

In 1870 Edison established an "invention factory," a forerunner of the research labs that most corporations operate today. He continued working on improvements to the telegraph and other instruments, including Alexander Graham Bell's recent invention, the telephone. In 1877 he invented the phonograph. Two years later he found ways to make the incandescent lightbulb, the kind we use today, commercially practical.

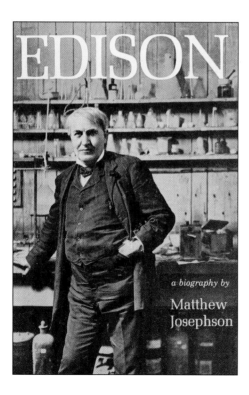

Thomas Edison is perhaps the best known of all American inventors. Paradoxically, he is really most important for developing the ideas of others, not producing them himself. However, he deserves credit for working out the first sound recording device. Here, the book jacket for one of the many biographies of Edison.

But perhaps Edison's most important work was in developing a system for producing and distributing large quantities of electricity cheaply over long distances. His dynamos opened up vast possibilities in wiring whole cities for electric lights, electric trolley cars, and perhaps most important of all, electric motors. With steam power, one huge steam engine drove many machines via pulleys and belts that had to be run all through a factory. Now individual electric motors could be attached to each machine, eliminating the system of belts and pulleys, and allowing much more flexibility in setting up a factory.

Despite his reputation, Edison was not a great genius coming up with new scientific principles and discoveries. Aside from the phonograph, most of his work was in developing, and making practical, ideas conceived by others. Nonetheless, his effect on modern life was powerful.

Fueled by the incoming flood of people and the new technologies, cities began to spread, almost visibly swallowing up fields, forests, and farms. In order to do so, they needed yet other new technologies. As we have seen, the old walking cities were small and close-knit, with people's homes within walking distance of their jobs. Merchants lived in city centers near the offices and warehouses; the middle class lived in a circle around the downtown center; and laborers lived on the outskirts.

But as the cities spread it was no longer convenient, or even possible, for people to walk to work, to the shops, to docks, and railroad stations. They needed faster ways of getting around. The first solutions to public transportation were "omnibuses," horse-drawn, roofed wagons with rows of benches, which could carry twenty or thirty people. The omnibuses improved public transportation somewhat, but they were slow and sometimes had trouble maneuvering through the growing downtown traffic.

Then, in the late 1840s, a way was found to lay railroad tracks flush with the road surface. Trolleys, drawn by horses, could move much faster along rails, and the horse-drawn trolley became the major form of city transportation. By 1880 there were 19,000 horse-drawn streetcars in use, and virtually every city of over 50,000 population had its system.

With the development of the electric dynamo, the horse trolleys were converted to electricity. Power lines were strung in webs over thousands of miles of city streets, and the trolley car became a major feature of American cities. Between 1888, when Boston introduced the first electric trolley system, and 1895, 85 percent of all the old horse-drawn trolleys had been electrified. Everyone used them, rich and poor alike. Trolleys were still operating in a few American cities a hundred years later, and they are even today an important part of the transportation network in many cities in Europe. Indeed, so efficient were the electric trolley systems that there is talk today of reintroducing them in several cities, including Los Angeles, where automobile pollution is a serious problem.

The final step in developing the modern mass transit system for cities also came as a result of the development of electric power. The idea of putting trains underground where they were out of heavy traffic was not new, but steam trains choked tunnels with steam and coal smoke. Elevated railroads running above street traffic were tried in New York and elsewhere, but they were noisy, dirty, expensive to build, and darkened the streets below them.

Electric power made subways feasible. The first subway was built in London in 1890. Boston began building its subway system in 1895; New York started in 1904 what would become a huge subway system of 722 miles, emblematic of the city. Young New Yorkers today are riding to school on the same subway lines that carried their parents, grandparents, even great-grandparents.

The creation of mass transit systems of various kinds changed the shape of cities. Trolley lines generally radiated outward from city centers to the outskirts like spokes of a wheel. In some cases promoters actually built amusement parks and athletic grounds at the end of trolley lines to increase business on the trolleys. Previously, businessmen and the middle

The horse-drawn trolley was the first really successful system of mass public transportation put into use in American cities. As can be seen from this photograph, horse trolleys continued in use well into the twentieth century, when cars and trucks were already taking over the streets.

By the 1880s electric-powered trolleys were beginning to replace horse-drawn ones. Note the grilled bumper in front of the trolley that could clear debris—and animals—from the tracks.

class generally had wanted to live in the city centers to be within walking distances of their offices. With the new mass transit systems they could get to work easily from the outskirts. Many chose to build large houses with spacious grounds for their families at the edge of their cities.

In this fashion there arose a significant aspect of American life, the suburb. These early suburbs were within city boundaries, usually one to three miles from the city center, and were sometimes called "streetcar suburbs." City downtowns became less residential. Business offices, shops, hotels, banks, government buildings, etc. grew where once there had been houses and apartment buildings.

As a consequence, laboring people tended to move into the downtown areas, often finding places to live near warehouses and factories. In some cases formerly elegant neighborhoods became homes to workers, as for example New York's Greenwich Village, where in the latter years of the 1880s six-story tenement buildings replaced two- and three-story middle-class homes.

The importance of technology to the growing cities did not end with transportation. As their populations soared, it became obvious that they would have to grow upward as well as outward. However, buildings of brick or stone could go only so high: The higher they went, the greater weight the lower floors had to carry. This meant that the lower walls had to be very thick to bear the weight, sharply reducing the interior space. Then in 1848 New York inventor James Bogardus designed a building supported by cast-iron columns inside. He then began building factories and warehouses supported entirely by cast-iron girders instead of brick or stone. Such buildings could be eight stories or more in height, and many were built in cities like Philadelphia, Chicago, Baltimore, and New York. Some of them are still in use today.

But a building taller than five or six stories meant a very long climb. It was obvious to everybody that buildings could only rise so high unless there was some way of transporting people rapidly up and down them.

The idea of an elevator was very old, but elevators had always been considered dangerous. Then in 1853 Elisha G. Otis worked out a safety device to keep an elevator from racing downward if the cable broke. Now there was virtually no limit to the height of buildings.

The final step in the creation of the modern big-city skyscraper came in the 1880s, when William Le Baron Jenney designed a ten-story building in Chicago. The heart of the building was a steel frame bolted together, which could then be covered with almost any kind of material. The steel frame was self-supporting—it could stand on its own. The system was sometimes called "the iron cage and the curtain wall." This new method, combined with the elevator, made buildings of almost any height possible. Through the 1890s and into the twentieth century there was a boom in skyscraper building, and the great city skylines of today began to rise over harbors and prairies. The early skyscrapers were usually covered with stone; today glass or metals like aluminum are frequently used.

The modern industrial city was thus the result of several forces work-

Many cast-iron buildings are still in use in American cities. Cast iron could easily be molded into decorative shapes, and as this picture shows, cast-iron buildings often had quite elaborate facades, of interest to students of design today.

Improved types of steel made steel-frame construction possible. A self-supporting frame was built, and then sheathed in stone, metal, glass, or brick. The height of steel frame buildings is virtually unlimited. This picture shows the construction in 1970-74 of Chicago's 110-story Sears Tower.

ing together: The rise of industry, the movement of large numbers of people from rural areas in both America and Europe, and the new technologies. By 1910 the old rural America was gone for the great majority of Americans. In its place was a nation of cities, some great, some small, as it still is today.

It is important for us to understand that cities are not simply masses of people living close together. Cities have "dynamics" of their own, which are different from the dynamics of small towns and farm areas.

For one thing, cities encouraged a great upwelling of what we often call "culture." Cities promoted the growth of the great newspapers that are such a part of modern life. There had been newspapers in America from as early as the colonial period, but even back in the eighteenth century, newspapers had been published in cities where copies could easily be distributed to readers living within walking distance of printing presses. But the explosion of the cities allowed newspapers to reach tens of thousands, even millions of readers who lived close at hand. Even today there are few national newspapers: Most are published city by city, like the *Cleveland Plain Dealer*, the *St. Louis Post-Dispatch*, the *Los Angeles Times*.

In addition to newspapers, museums, theaters, and concert halls were located in cities—even if some were rather small cities. It was possible to build a museum, concert hall, or theater in the countryside; but what was the point of it, if people could get to them only with difficulty? Museums, concert halls, and research libraries sprang up in cities because there were plenty of people nearby to use them. Not surprisingly, the second half of

By the mid-nineteenth century many cities sported lavish theaters, dance halls, and open-air entertainment gardens. This picture shows one of the most famous of them, Niblo's Garden, in New York City.

the 1800s saw a huge boom in the construction of the great museums and concert halls that are a major feature of our cities.

Similarly, cities also fostered the growth of the extraordinary entertainment industry that is so important to modern life. Before the city boom, most entertainment was homemade—a dance to Uncle Ned's fiddle, cornhusking parties and quilting bees, singing around the parlor piano. But with large numbers of people tied together in cities by mass transportation systems, it was easy to gather large crowds for shows, circuses, plays, dances, and, later on, movies.

So it was with sports. So long as most Americans lived on farms and in small towns, a horse race, wrestling match, or ballgame could attract at best a few hundred spectators, not enough to make such an event very

As these old baseball cards indicate, sporting teams were built around cities. Pittsburgh's Honus Wagner was one of the greatest of all shortstops. Cleveland's Nap Lajoie led the American League in hitting four straight years. Chicago's Mordecai "Three-Fingers" Brown was a star pitcher of his time.

profitable. Sports were almost entirely homemade by amateurs. But in cities it was possible to gather crowds of thousands, or even tens of thousands. By 1900 there were major-league baseball teams in most big cities east of the Mississippi and minor-league teams in other cities and towns elsewhere. Horse racing was becoming a major sport, and college football was attracting attention. Sports, like entertainment, were becoming big business centered in the cities.

The city, with its own dynamic, actually changed much about the way people lived their lives. But in an even more subtle way, it changed the way people thought, too. To begin with, on the farms and in country villages, life was regulated by the sun and the moon, and weather was a daily matter of critical importance: A day's activities had to take weather into account. But workers in the factories and offices at the big cities ran their lives by clocks, and weather was simply a minor nuisance.

Again, on the farms there was always something to do: Farm wives worked as much as eighty hours a week. City dwellers, even those working sixty hours a week, had more leisure time, and that leisure time increased as working hours were reduced. This extra leisure time, of course, benefited the actors, musicians, theater owners, promoters, and thousands of others who were developing the new entertainment business.

Beyond all of this, the city actually changed the ways people felt as they went about their daily business. In rural areas people might spend days at a stretch seeing few others outside of their families. They tended to have close relations with a small number of people, mostly parents, children, brothers and sisters, cousins, uncles and aunts. At the one-room schoolhouses they walked to they rarely saw more than twenty to thirty students of all ages from four to sixteen. In cities people spent the bulk of their days among casual acquaintances, in huge schools and factories often with outright strangers, like the customers clerks in shops waited on, or the passengers trolley conductors collected tickets from. Families were less tightly bonded, with the members separating to go to different jobs and schools in the morning, separating again in the evening to do homework, visit friends, go to shows and concerts.

The city, then, was not merely a whole lot of people living close together. It was something new–and it drastically changed the way of American life.

CHAPTER IV

City Problems

I t is not in the nature of things that so sweeping a change as the rise of the cities would take place without problems. And problems there were, of all sorts—garbage heaped in the streets, impure water, millions of newcomers unable to speak English, inadequate fire and police forces, and more.

Most of these problems did not exist for country people. For example, in the country, people disposed of their garbage by feeding it to the pigs or simply throwing it into the fields and woods, where it was eaten by wild animals or quickly rotted. Country people used privies, or "outhouses," for toilets, which could be moved as necessary. In the country water was plentiful; each house had its own individual well, as many still do today. Fires did burn down houses and barns, but with farms scattered, a fire in one building did not spread to others, as they did in cities. Nor was there any need for organized police forces in country villages: A bad actor could be brought to heel by the local constable with a little help from his neighbors very quickly.

Most of these early fire departments were clubs of volunteers, as indeed are many rural fire departments today. Inevitably, they did not work as efficiently as modern professional fire departments.

As cities developed from villages and towns in the 1700s and 1800s, city dwellers continued country practices, using privies in cellars or backyards, and tossing their garbage in the streets. But now there were ten, or fifty, or a hundred people living in the space formerly occupied by one farm family; the refuse, along with other problems, multiplied. The streets filled with garbage, and pigs were let run wild in the streets to consume the litter. Manure left by horses and other animals might be left to fester for weeks. Philip Hone, a former mayor of New York, said in 1832 that the city was "one huge pigsty," which it undoubtedly was.

As in the country, water was drawn either from the rivers or streams that the cities were built on, or from wells dug as they were in the country. But a lot of refuse was being washed into those rivers, and poison from garbage was seeping into the wells. Inevitable, there was much disease; epidemics of smallpox, cholera, and other illnesses swept cities from time to time.

Fire departments were run by amateur fire companies for the most part. But some cities had private fire companies that would come to your house only if you were a subscriber who had paid in advance. Policing was done mainly by badly paid watchmen who were usually no match for well-armed criminals. There were no such things as detective squads, or until the mid-nineteenth century, even uniformed police. (The first uniformed police force organized on a semimilitary basis was established in New York City in 1844. Other cities quickly followed this model.) Criminals were everywhere.

Then, as immigrants from abroad and newcomers from American farms began to flood into the cities, everything worsened. Denser populations made it easier for disease to spread, and put greater strain on sanitation facilities and water supplies. Slums seemed to spring up naturally in cities when they reached a certain size. By the 1830s there were slums in New York City and soon they were festering in American cities everywhere.

A "slum" is not a simple problem, but a complex of problems that feed on one another. Overcrowding, crime, disease, alcoholism, poverty, prostitution, broken homes, drug addiction, unemployment, child abuse, and violence are all worse in slums than they are elsewhere. As with the proverbial chicken and the egg, it is always difficult to discover which comes first—that is to say, what exactly is the root cause of the slum problem.

The slums of New York City are a classic example. The city was founded at the southern end of the famous Manhattan Island, and spread northward, as the wealthy and the middle class sought open spaces for their houses. New arrivals, most of them poor, tended to settle in the

The problem of street cleaning lingered throughout the 1800s and is, in fact, still with us today. Here slum children play in a gutter, ignoring the dead horse, a sight they were very used to.

older areas where the jobs were. Landlords quickly saw that there was money to be made in cutting up buildings into tiny apartments. New buildings, often little more than shacks, were thrown up in backyards, creating "an intricate array of dark, foul courts and alleys." The shortage of housing allowed landlords to rent basements and attics for good prices. An 1843 survey showed that 7,196 New Yorkers were living in cellars. By 1850 the number had increased fourfold.

One notorious tenement, at 36 Cherry Street, had five hundred people living on five floors—about a hundred people in the space found today in about four suburban homes. There was no heat or running water in the building.

Slum tenants, most of them newcomers from the farms and immigrants from Europe, often took in boarders to meet the high rents. Frequently two or three families would be jammed into a three- or four-room apartment. Few people in tenements had their own beds: Children slept three or four to a bed, and even adults doubled up. In some cases a worker on a night shift might occupy a bed in the day that was used at night by somebody on the day shift.

As newcomers poured into cities from the countryside and abroad, the demand for housing grew rapidly. Landlords began pulling down the two- and three-story houses (left) that had been typical of cities, replacing them with five- and six-story dumbbell tenements (right) that might eventually house a hundred people on a plot of ground on which a single family had formerly lived. Ironically, some of these tenements, now located in expensive downtown areas, today get high rents, as for example these tenements (right) in New York's desirable Greenwich Village area.

Overcrowding by itself may not have been the root cause of slum conditions—historians are not sure about that—but it certainly worsened them. Sanitation was almost nonexistent; a dozen families might share a backyard or basement privy and one water pump. In these conditions, infectious diseases were more easily passed around. To escape the confines of the tenement, especially in the baking heat of summer, children ran unsupervised in the streets. Boys formed into gangs with names like the Blood Tubs, Dead Rabbits, Plug-Uglies. Such gangs fought, stole, drank, and terrorized neighborhoods.

As significant as the physical problems were the emotional ones. Many of the slum dwellers lived without much hope that their lives would ever improve. True, Americans have always had the belief that people who worked hard and maybe had a bit of luck could move "up and out," as the saying was. In fact, millions did just that, starting perhaps as street vendors or junk collectors and building small businesses into bigger ones. But it is also true that millions never escaped the slums. Slum dwellers often could not see a way out for themselves. Sensing that they were trapped, some turned to crime and prostitution to pay the bills, or to alcohol and drugs to raise their spirits.

As cities grew rapidly through the first decades of the 1800s, it was abundantly clear that these problems had to be tackled. Cities began arranging for a supply of pure water early. In 1801 Philadelphia installed its Central Square Water Works. It quickly became inadequate, and in 1822 the city built the Fairmount Water Works. In 1835 New York started to build a vast system of tunnels that would bring in water from the Croton Reservoir forty miles north of the city. It was completed in 1842 and had to be greatly enlarged only sixteen years later. Other cities followed suit, and by the beginning of the Civil War in 1860 there were sixty-eight public water systems operating in American cities.

Other problems were not so easily solved. Garbage was one of them: The rapidly growing cities simply could not handle the massive amounts of waste city dwellers generated every day. Chicago made a heroic effort to cope, actually reversing the course of the Chicago River so that garbage would be carried off to the Illinois River and thence into the Mississippi, rather than Lake Michigan. Nonetheless, in 1880 the *Chicago Times* said, "The river stinks. The air stinks. People's clothing permeated by the foul atmosphere stinks...." Finally, by the later years of the 1800s the situation was improved as sewer systems were dug and garbage was more regularly collected. Yet in truth, the problem of disposing of city waste is still with us today, as cities find themselves shipping garbage hundreds of miles for disposal.

Ridding cities of slums proved to be an even more intractable problem. One major problem was the old American belief that governments ought not to interfere with property rights—in this case the right of a landlord to do whatever he wanted with his buildings. According to this line of thought, governments should not require landlords to improve their buildings simply for the good of their tenants.

But by the 1840s many people had concluded that something had to be done. Progress was slow, but in 1860 New York City passed a law requiring tenements to have fire escapes. Thereafter various laws established standards for room size, ventilation, sanitation, and other matters. These laws only scratched the surface: Millions of city dwellers continued to live in squalid, even dangerous, conditions. But it was a start.

Then in 1879 the infamous "dumbbell" tenement was devised in New York. The dumbbell tenement had an indentation in each side a few feet deep and perhaps twenty feet long. When several of these buildings were lined up side by side they would leave "airshafts" five feet wide running from top to bottom. Inside rooms, like kitchens and bedrooms, faced on these airshafts, providing the rooms with at least some light and fresh air. These dumbbell tenements were five or six stories high and took up nearly all of a 25- by 100-foot lot. Each floor had two three-room and two four-room apartments. There were supposed to be two toilets on each floor, shared by two apartments. Ironically, these dumbbell tenements, which were planned to improve matters by providing light and air to all the rooms, became notoriously overcrowded. They spread across New York "like a scab," as somebody said. They had solved nothing.

But at least people now agreed that city governments had to step in and take charge if the problems of cities were ever to be solved. And through the 1890s and into the 1900s all over America city housing became more tightly regulated. Eventually landlords were required to supply heat, toilets, running water, fire protection, and in general upgrade city housing. Even today there is still room for improvement; but we have come a long way from the dismal tenements like the one on Cherry Street.

Many people believed that one good way to help improve slum conditions was through education. It was believed that slum children who could not read and write English, did not know basic arithmetic, and were ignorant of simple rules of health and nutrition would have difficulty getting along in the world, would inevitably remain in poverty, and would easily become lured into crime, drugs, alcoholism. Through education such children might be helped to rise.

In earlier years, outside of New England, American education had been informal and haphazard. Wealthy people and the small middle class generally sent their children to various types of private schools. But the bulk of children, growing up as they did on farms, were often prevented from attending school by weather and work. Not until the 1870s was an elementary education available to many American children living in the countryside—though they often had to walk miles to get it.

In cities, however, as was the case in so many other matters, it was more feasible to provide education for at least the younger children—there were, after all, scores of them living on every block. Many of these children, as we have seen, were running loose. A belief grew that they ought to be in school learning their ABC's and the times tables rather

Slum children were expected to work from early ages by their impoverished families. They were in demand because they could be paid less. This was particularly true of textile factories, like this one, because their small fingers were adept at tying knots necessary to the spinning of thread.

than getting their education in the streets.

The real push for public education came with the beginnings of significant immigration after 1820. City fathers grew concerned that immigrants did not understand American ideals, principles, folkways, and in most cases the English language. If they were to make their way in America they would at least have to be able to read and write English. Through the 1840s and 1850s cities increasingly made education available to young people. New York City created its Board of Education in 1842. By the 1850s Boston's leaders were insisting that education was essential to "securing urban order and stability." So in cities everywhere schools were built and teachers were hired.

But inevitably there were problems. For one thing, schools' budgets, as they have often been in America, were frequently inadequate, leaving one teacher in a classroom of fifty or sixty students. For another, Roman Catholics felt that public education was biased toward Protestantism, and wanted their own schools. For a third, many of the immigrants were suspicious of American schools, which they felt would draw the children away from their parents' cultures. Finally, poor families needed their children to work in order to bring in a few more pennies each week. The result was that in 1860 in New York City only about a third of the city's children were in school on any given day. The situation was much the same in other cities. Children of the cities were getting a spotty and haphazard education at best, and many of them were getting no education at all. On the other hand, it was in the cities that the first high schools were established, and by the mid-1900s you could get a better education in most cities than you could in the rural towns.

Nobody had expected that well-engineered water and sewer systems, the dumbbell tenements, and improved public school systems would cure all the ills of the city. But reformers had thought that these new schemes would improve conditions for city dwellers, especially those living in the tenements. But the improvement, if any, was not large. By the 1870s, it was clear that something was still wrong. People shouldn't have to live as they did in the tenements, nor should middle-class families have to put up with the ignorance and criminality spawned in the slums. Reformers began to question the policy of laissez-faire that prevented government from intervening to remedy the physically and socially unhealthy conditions. In the decades after the Civil War, a great majority of city dwellers came to agree.

CHAPTER V

The Failure of City Government

Many of the problems of government, as we have seen, were simply physical—that is, developing a good supply of pure water, removing the mountains of refuse that piled up every day, providing decent housing for working people, developing competent police and fire departments.

But underlying these difficulties were more basic problems. Cities had, by and large, grown out of small towns, or even villages. Obviously, a small town does not need a lot of governmental machinery, just a mayor or board of selectmen, a few judges, and a small number of officials to collect taxes, supervise the schools, see that roads are kept up.

As these American towns grew into cities, governmental machinery was increased bit by bit, haphazardly. Rarely did anyone sit down and work out a new plan for city government. As a consequence, by the second half of the 1800s most cities were being run by governments that were simply bigger versions of small-town governments. In some cases there were mayors and councils, but no commissions for water, sewage, street construction, bridge repair, and so forth. All of these jobs were handled by the mayor and council, most of whom had no special expertise in dealing with water or sewage.

In other places the problem was just the opposite: There were a whole lot of departments and boards, each responsible for its own area—health, streets, fire, police, water, and the rest of it—but with little or no central control. One city had fourteen different boards of this kind. In some cities each board could send out its own tax bills; in other cases only the central government could tax, and the boards and departments had to beg for money. In general, there was poor fiscal control of taxes and expenditures.

Inevitably, in some cases nobody would accept responsibility. There

Manhattan's early reservoir located in Central Park soon proved inadequate for the rapidly growing population. In time an extensive system of reservoirs connected to the city by aqueducts were built in outlying areas.

were no city planners. Department heads were often people with no experience who had got their jobs because they were political allies of the mayor or political boss. When a different political party took over, a new set of department heads, even less experienced, would take over. Confusion reigned everywhere, and of course there were always corrupt politicians around to take advantage of the situation.

This might all have been bad enough; but adding to the disorder was a second wave of immigrants, beginning in about 1880, pouring into the cities, mostly in the Northeast, but to some extent everywhere. These immigrants were somewhat different from the earlier wave, who had been mainly German and Irish. They still came; but now there was a huge influx of immigrants from Southern and Eastern Europe. Particularly large numbers of Italians, especially from Southern Italy, and Jews from Russia and Poland poured in during this period. In addition, by the 1880s there was beginning to be significant immigration from China and somewhat later Japan, mainly into western cities, but also into cities everywhere.

Like the earlier immigrants, these new arrivals had been driven out by harsh landlords, high taxes, farm problems, and political upheaval. They, too, were drawn to America as a land of great abundance where there seemed to be jobs for everybody—where indeed, they believed, anyone could get rich. (For a full discussion of American immigration see the volume in this series called *A Century of Immigration 1820–1924*.)

The first Italians to come, as was frequently the case, were single young men looking for jobs. Many of these young Italian men came over in the spring to work at the construction trades—often building the very tenements their fellow immigrants would occupy—and then went home in the fall with a pocketful of dollars. In the end, almost half of Italian immigrants went home. But the other half did not. Between 1880 and 1913 more than 4.1 million Italians entered America. No other ethnic group ever came in so large numbers in so brief a time. Very quickly there grew up in American cities, especially in the Northeast, Little Italys where Italian was spoken, saints' days celebrated, pasta eaten.

Jews, too, came in large numbers, but only a small percentage went back, or had any wish to do so. Most immigrants endured one or another sort of hardship at home that propelled them toward the United States, but many of the Jews in Europe faced physical violence, beatings, and even death. While the Jews came from everywhere, the largest number originally lived in what was known as the Pale, a huge area of Poland and Russia, which at various times had belonged to Lithuania as well as to the other two nations. Jews were treated as

This famous picture of Italian immigrants arriving at Ellis Island was taken by Lewis Hine, who was noted for documenting city life, particularly immigrants and the slums they so often inhabited.

inferior citizens. At times they could not own land, but lived in shtetels or little villages, often working at trades like butchering, baking, tailoring.

As ever, there were substantial differences between all immigrant groups—Italians, Germans, Jews, Irish, Chinese, Polish, and so many others. Jews had a strong tradition of education, based on an ancient respect for learned men who studied Jewish religious books; they tended to keep their children in school as long as they could afford to, although like most immigrants, struggling families usually needed their children to go to work early. By contrast, many immigrants from Southern Italy felt that American schools undercut the authority of parents and turned children away from the old culture, and for other reasons did not encourage their children to stay in school. The Irish were resolutely city dwellers; many of the Germans became farmers. The immigrants worshiped in very different ways as. Catholics, Protestants, Jews, with smaller numbers of Buddhists, Muslims, and other religions mixed in. They of course spoke many languages—German, Jews, and Chinese did not even use the same alphabet. They had their own habits of dress, their own holidays, their own diets: Consider the differences between traditional Jewish, Chinese, and Italian food, all of which Americans are familiar with today.

Integrating these diverse groups into one community was a formidable task, and as most of the immigrants lived in cities, it was a problem left to city governments, not the states or the federal government, to solve. (Even today big-city mayors complain that the federal government sets rules for who can come to America in what numbers, but leaves it to the cities to provide help for them once they are here.) Many immigrants coped successfully with conditions in their new land; but many found the differences they were faced with bewildering.

Inevitably misunderstanding arose; there was friction, which in time led to turf wars between ethnic gangs trying to keep others out of their streets and neighborhoods. Diversity is a widely admired idea in the United States today; but there is also no doubt that ethnic groups living side by side do not always manage to get along peacefully.

The immigrants, however, were hardly responsible for all the ills of the cities: Many of the problems, like water supply, fire prevention, garbage disposal, and outdated government systems, had existed long before most of the immigrants arrived. But unquestionably, trying to integrate millions of newcomers with different ways into cities was an added burden for city governments, especially when those governments were not adequately set up to deal with problems of any kind.

As always, when there is a power vacuum, somebody will step in to fill it. This was what happened in the cities. Smart, often unscrupulous politicians began to see ways for making themselves rich with the help of the tenement dwellers, increasing numbers of whom were immigrants living in their Germantowns, Little Italys, and Chinatowns. An informal, often only half-understood, bargain was made: The local politician—often an immigrant or son of immigrants himself—would help struggling immigrants with their problems; and in return the immigrants would vote for the politician or his candidates. The local politician would see to it that newcomers were registered to vote, often illegally. He would speak to a judge he was friendly with—indeed may have got elected—about being lenient with a boy who had got into trouble. He would see to it that his people got a fair share of city jobs sweeping the streets, shoveling snow, working in the parks. He would help a widow with the paperwork so she could get charitable aid.

These local politicians soon made themselves powerful in their wards, or political districts, and neighborhoods. From there they went on to take over other neighborhoods, or make alliances with other local politicians. The end result was that many American cities effectively came to be run by a "boss" or a small clique of bosses who controlled enough votes to elect mayors, aldermen, councilmen, and the like.

The most infamous of these city bosses was New York's William

Marcy Tweed. There had existed since the 1790s in New York the Tammany Club, which became allied to the Democratic Party. The club was influential, and New York politicians often consulted Tammany Hall about whom to run for office. Tweed's father, who was not an immigrant, was a craftsman who had been treasurer of the Tammany Club. Tweed himself began his career as leader of a local gang, then became head of a volunteer fire company at a time when fire companies were politically powerful. Tammany leaders felt that young Tweed showed promise, got him elected to the city council and then to Congress. By the 1860s Tweed had got control of Tammany Hall. He used his position to gain control not only of the New York City government but of some state legislators as well. The Tweed "ring" was carefully organized through a system of ward captains and lesser politicians—many of them leaders of immigrant groups—who dealt with the individual voters in their own neighborhoods. Soon Tweed was the biggest of all big-city bosses and he set about enriching himself and his friends.

There were several ways money could be extracted from the system. In some cases people with city jobs were expected to

The celebrated William Marcy Tweed, best known of all big-city bosses, posed for this portrait, which was intended to make him appear a figure of elegance, but left him looking like the criminal he proved to be.

pay a percentage of their salaries to the political ring. This alone could bring in millions of dollars a year. A more common scheme was for people who wanted to do business with the city to "kick back" to the politicians part of their profits. For example, suppose the city decided to put in a swimming pool in a certain area. The contractors who dug the hole, who poured the foundation, who laid the tiles, who installed the water pipes were allowed to overcharge for their services, sometimes two, three, or even ten times as much as necessary. In exchange, they would give the politicians a substantial part of their corrupt earnings.

Yet another way politicians and their friends could benefit from holding office was through real estate speculation. It went like this: Suppose the city planned to put in a new park. Before word got out, the politicians and their friends would buy up all the land proposed for the park site, and often the land nearby. Once the park was started, the value of the land would quickly rise, and the politicians would sell out at a considerable profit. (One politician of the time called this "honest graft," as opposed to kickbacks, which he considered "dishonest graft.")

The amount of money that ended up in politicians' pockets was astonishing. A courthouse built while Tweed was New York's boss was budgeted at $250,000; its final cost was $13 million, over fifty times the original estimate—money that ended up in the hands of Tweed, his associates, and the contractors. City bosses had to spread this graft around to keep people loyal to them, but they kept plenty for themselves. Boss Tweed had a mansion on Fifth Avenue, an estate in Connecticut, a steam yacht, a stable of fine horses, and millions of dollars hidden away.

The political machines worked somewhat differently from city to city. Chicago, for example, in the era we are looking at never had a supreme boss on the order of Tweed in New York. This may have been due to the way the city sprawled across the prairie, or perhaps its rapid growth, or some other factor. There were in Chicago several machines controlling various aspects of the city at various times. Sometimes they joined forces, sometimes they fought. But for the taxpayer the net result was always the same. In Philadelphia, for example, between 1860 and 1880 the city debt soared from $20 million to $70 million.

Some historians believe that these big-city political machines performed an important and necessary service. These bosses needed the votes of the slum dwellers and the poor generally, who constituted a major portion of the voters, most of them, but by no means all, immigrants. They were more aware of the problems of such people than were the wealthy and middle-class people who dominated business, finance, and to some extent, despite the bosses, government. The local ward boss would bring food baskets to the hungry and coal to impoverished families in winter;

While there is no doubt that the big-city political machines did come to the aid of some individual poor, they left the basic problems untouched. This photograph by Jacob Riis, whose pictures of slum life were important to awakening Americans to the problem, shows two homeless boys, barefoot and clad in dirty, ragged clothes. Thousands of children like these wandered American streets while politicians looked the other way.

he provided jobs for the able-bodied, and saw to it that the sick got medical services. Furthermore, in order to increase the potential for graft, the political machines built a lot of bridges, parks, bathhouses, and courthouses that otherwise might never have existed. The public projects not only made life more convenient for poor city dwellers but also created thousands of jobs as well.

It is nonetheless true that the cost was inordinate. The parks and bridges could have been built and the poor served much more cheaply without the machines. And while the machines may have helped individual immigrants, the poor, and the slum dwellers to find city jobs or get a child out of trouble, they did nothing at all to attack the root problems of poverty and the slums. The corrupt politicians who aided some individuals hurt many more. One historian has written: "A woman whose family enjoyed [the machine's] Christmas turkey might be widowed by an accident to her husband in a sweatshop kept open by a timely bribe. Filthy buildings might claim her children, as corrupt inspectors ignored serious violations."

Perhaps even more significantly, the machine system undermined the essence of democracy. The system allowed the bosses, not the people, to decide who held office and how tax money was spent. By the 1870s— after two or three decades of exploding cities—all of this was becoming clear, and once again thoughtful people were beginning to conclude that things had to change.

CHAPTER VI

Reform

The reform movement that swept America, beginning in about 1870, had profound effects not only for the cities but for the nation as a whole. The massive plundering of city treasuries by the bosses and their machines, the crime and squalor of the slums, and the inefficient sanitation, transport, fire, and police systems were too obvious to be ignored anymore. Everybody was being hurt—the middle class and well-to-do through the wasting of their tax money, the poor through the miserable and unhealthy conditions in which they had to live and work.

Very important in triggering the reform movement were the writings of the "muckrakers," a group of journalists who reported on the misdeeds of the machine bosses and the problems of the cities generally. The best known of the muckrakers was Lincoln Steffens, a highly educated man who began reporting on corruption in city governments in the 1890s. In 1904 he published *The Shame of the Cities*, based on his newspaper and magazine reporting. This book was widely read and discussed,

Two of the most important writers on social problems—the muckrakers—were Lincoln Steffens, speaking at a demonstration, and Ida Tarbell, shown in 1904 when she was at the height of her fame.

and confirmed what city dwellers already knew, that the bosses were stealing millions from the taxpayers.

A second well-known muckraker was Ida Tarbell, first recognized for her attack on the monopolistic practices of John D. Rockefeller's Standard Oil Company, which had got a stranglehold on the oil industry and was cheating the public through overcharges and other devices. The works of Tarbell, Steffens, and other muckrakers gave weight to the drive for reform.

In the opinion of reformers, sweeping changes to city government systems were needed. For one thing, cities had grown out of towns and villages that had originally been set up when the states had a great deal to say about what town and village governments could and could not do. A hundred years later the state governments still held that power.

Unfortunately for the city, by the late nineteenth century, most state legislatures were malapportioned, so that there were far more legislators from rural areas, and far fewer from the cities, than there should have been in terms of population and fair representation. The rural legislators tended to dislike cities, which they saw as breeding grounds for crime and corruption. They were unwilling to do more for cities, or spend more on them then they had to.

JACOB RIIS

Although not usually classified with the muckrakers, Jacob Riis had a profound effect on the public with his book *How the Other Half Lives*. Riis was an immigrant from Denmark, where he had grown up in a small town quite different from the big city he had immigrated to in 1870. After trying a number of jobs, he ended up in journalism. For thirteen years he was a New York City police reporter, frequently covering crimes in slum areas, like the Lower East Side. As an immigrant, he was particularly sympathetic to other immigrants, most of them far worse off than he was. He was a pioneering photographer of city scenes. His book contained dozens of pictures of life in the slums, many of them shocking, even today. From these pictures many middle-class Americans gained their first knowledge of the poverty that surrounded them. Some of Riis' pictures appear in the book you are reading.

For a second matter, the old towns had usually been set up so that power lay in the hands of a council, a board of eldermen, leaving little authority for the mayor. The councilmen were usually elected one from each ward, or in some similar way. In order to stay in office they had to provide things for the voters in their wards, and this often involved bribery and kickbacks. Too often, ward bosses quarreled among themselves, and their failure to cooperate left city administration in a shambles. It seemed to the reformers that the system was bound to be corrupt.

At the turn of the twentieth century, industrialists were consolidating smaller corporations into huge industrial empires, like Rockefeller's Standard Oil, J.P. Morgan's U.S. Steel, and his enormous banking combine. These corporations were providing millions of jobs, producing vast quantities of goods, and spinning off enormous profits for the people who owned them. They seemed to be the very definition of success. Later on it was discovered that much of the success of these mammoth corporations had come from sheer ruthlessness and dubious, even illegal methods. But at the time the great industrialists were much admired.

Many reformers came to believe that cities ought to be run like corporations, with a chain of command leading to one farsighted man at the top. This was not surprising, for the reform leaders tended to be drawn from the middle class, especially the well-to-do who had the leisure to put time into fighting for change. Many of these people were decision makers in corporations or owned stock in them, and naturally looked to the industrial giants as models.

The basic idea of the reformers, then, was to run the cities as corporations were run, with an eye to efficiency and good order, relying on trained technicians to supervise public utilities and other tax-supported functions. Beginning in about 1870, city charters were rewritten to give mayors increasing authority at the expense of city councils. Some mayors gained the right to veto council actions. Various administrative boards with overlapping tasks were streamlined, often with some of their powers being handed over to the mayor. For example, in 1882 under a new charter, Brooklyn (then an independent city) ended the council's right to approve the mayor's appointments. This was important, for it meant that councilmen could no longer hand out city jobs to their supporters. Of course the mayor could, but it was a lot easier for the public to keep an eye on one mayor than on twelve to thirty councilmen.

Still, when one political party defeated another at the polls and took over the city government, the new people usually threw out the office-holders who had been running school, sanitation, police, and other boards in order to give jobs to their supporters. Officeholders who had gained some experience in how to collect garbage or devise school curriculums were thus often replaced by people who knew little about the jobs they were supposed to be doing. In order to improve the situation, reformers pushed through laws that removed party names from ballots: You were to vote for the man, not the party. This way, it was hoped—vainly, as it turned out—party politics would be taken out of city government.

Another step in the same direction came in 1883, when the U.S. Congress passed the Pendleton Act. This new law set up a commission to control certain federal jobs, so they would go to the best-qualified people and not be doled out as political favors. Applicants for jobs would take examinations and could not be fired when control of the U.S. government changed hands.

Very quickly cities adopted this "civil service" idea. Milwaukee, Tacoma, Seattle, San Francisco and others put in civil service plans in the 1890s. The idea continued to spread thereafter. Not all city jobs were put under civil service, but a great many were; most city jobs today are run by civil service rules. True, civil service makes it harder to remove lazy or inefficient jobholders; but most experts believe that the advantages far outweigh the disadvantages.

Yet another reform was "initiative and referendum," first passed in

1898 in San Francisco. Under this scheme people did not have to wait for government officials to deal with a problem. A group could petition the government to permit a vote on a bill they wanted passed, and if a majority agreed it would become law, whether the city government approved or not.

A similar reform, started in Los Angeles, was "recall." Under this scheme voters could "deselect," or dismiss, an official they no longer approved of.

One more important reform came in 1913 when a constitutional amendment was passed requiring the direct election of senators. Until then, by the rules of the U.S. Constitution, senators had been chosen by state legislatures. As we have seen, because of malapportionment, rural legislators dominated state legislatures. These legislatures would inevitably choose senators biased against the cities. This in turn meant that the U.S. Senate had an antiurban attitude and was in no rush to provide cities with much help. With direct election, city voters, who by 1913 were the majority in many states, could elect U.S. senators more sympathetic to their needs. (As it turned out, unfortunately, city bosses often controlled these elections, too.)

Yet one more reform was impelled not by reformers but by forces of nature. In September 1900 a devastating hurricane slashed across Galveston, Texas. It brought with it a huge tidal wave that tore up bridges and smashed houses and buildings. Six thousand people died in the disaster, and a third of the city was ruined. It soon became clear that the demoralized city fathers were unable to cope with the situation. The state government stepped in. It set up a commission of five well-known local businessmen to govern during the emergency. The commission took great powers to itself, divided up the work among themselves and hired engineers and technicians to aid them. The commission turned out to be highly effective and soon Galveston was on the way to recovery.

So well did the system work that the Texas state legislature decided to keep it, and in 1903 it set up a permanent commission form of government for Galveston. Once again we see an effort made to run city government like a business. The commission idea quickly spread, encouraged by businessmen who believed that it would bring to their cities more efficient and less corrupt government. However, as one historian has said, commission government did not necessarily take politics out of government, nor increase efficiency: It "depended entirely upon finding the right candidates for election to the commission."

A second system meant to take politics out of city government was what is now known as the *city manager plan*. The point of this plan was

The Galveston flood of 1900, caused by a fierce hurricane, destroyed huge portions of the city. Houses like these were smashed into kindling, and thousands were left homeless as a result.

for a city to hire people with professional training to administer the city just as an executive would run a business. In 1908 the city of Staunton, Virginia, tried out the scheme with fair success. Then, after a disastrous flood struck Dayton, Ohio, that city also tried the city manager scheme. It worked well and thereafter the city manager system grew, until by 1926 over three hundred cities had managers, including large ones like Cincinnati, Cleveland, and Kansas City, Missouri. Mayors and councils were not eliminated, because most city charters required these elected officials. But departments of sanitation, fire, police, and more were left to the managers to run. Today, all across the country, thousands of cities—mostly small- and moderate- sized ones—use the city manager form of government.

The Dayton flood, which swept through the city, upsetting this streetcar and tearing up the streets, led to the introduction of the city manager system.

The reforms we have looked at were all governmental; but other reforms were carried out by private individuals. Perhaps the best known of these was the creation of the "settlement house," so called because it was aimed at helping newcomers to the city—mainly immigrants—to settle into their new world. The most famous of the settlement houses was Hull House in Chicago, started in 1889 by Jane Addams and Ellen Gates Starr. They bought an old mansion in the middle of an immigrant neighborhood, and opened a kindergarten for local children. Step by step they expanded the operation, until they were offering classes in English, music, cooking, sewing; presenting lectures and adult education courses; finding people jobs through an unemployment bureau; and performing many other services. The settlement house idea was not new; the first one had been founded in London, and there had been one in New York before Hull House in Chicago. But Hull House was the best known; and still exists today, although much changed. These early settlement houses were imitated in cities all over the nation. By 1895 there were at least fifty of them. There were many other private efforts at reform, including attempts, often by women, to teach slum women about child care, nutrition, health.

Beyond these, reformers pushed through a raft of building codes limiting the number of people who could live in a tenement, and requiring landlords to improve the heat, lighting, sanitary facilities, etc. in their buildings.

As we have seen, the push for reform came mainly from the middle class, and especially the well-to-do. Middle-class women were an important force among the reformers, in part because they had the leisure time and money to work on various types of committees, but also partly because of a sympathy they felt for the women living in terrible conditions in the slums.

Nonetheless, the people of the slums, who had much to gain by reform, were involved in the effort, too. Typical was the renowned Tim

Sullivan, a New York politician known throughout the city as "Big Tim." Born in poverty in 1863 and abandoned by his father, Sullivan was supported by a saintly mother who remained a great influence on him. Sullivan went to work as a newsboy at seven, rapidly moved up both in the newspaper distribution business and in politics. A handsome six-footer, he quickly became popular, and in his early twenties was picked to lead an assembly district that included the Bowery, an area of entertainment and vice peopled by many ethnic groups. In time Sullivan became one of the most powerful politicians in New York and eventually served in Congress.

Sullivan made a lot of money legitimately through a chain of vaudeville theaters. He also made money through illegal gambling interests. He is remembered today mainly as the sponsor of the famous Sullivan Law, the first attempt at gun control in New York State.

Sullivan was a typical big-city political boss. Nonetheless, he had a real concern for the slum people he had grown up among, and who cheered him on in election after election. In the late nineteenth century increasing numbers of women, particularly immigrant women, were working in "sweatshops," dirty, dark, unsafe, and sometimes unheated factories in slum areas. These women worked long hours in dreadful conditions. When reformers, many of them women, began fighting for laws to protect women workers from the worst abuses, Sullivan, who remembered what his mother had suffered in supporting a large family, threw himself into the fight on the side of the reformers. He helped the women to push through the state legislature one of the first important New York State laws aiding women workers.

We must remember that working people made up the majority of voters. Most of them were overworked and underpaid, and many of them were desperately poor. They were bound to support efforts to limit working hours; require factories to be safe, clean, and heated; force landlords to install toilets and running water. The votes of workers were crucial to

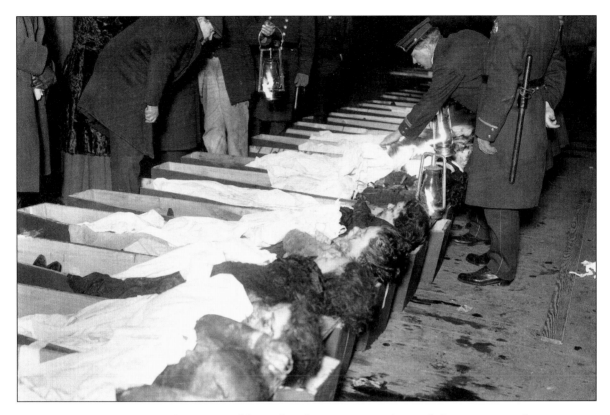

One of the most famous and horrific of America's industrial disasters was the fire at the Triangle Shirtwaist Factory in New York in 1911. Exit doors had been illegally locked and fire prevention equipment failed. The workers, mostly women, jumped from the windows eight stories above the streets, most of them to their deaths. The disaster awakened people to the conditions in the sweatshops and led to reforms. This picture shows bodies of victims being identified by relatives.

getting reforms passed. And there is also no doubt that some of the city bosses, like Big Tim Sullivan, helped in the effort.

But there is also no doubt that the reform leadership was drawn from the wealthier class. For one thing, they were usually better educated than the workers, and better understood what was wrong and how it could be fixed. For another, through their ownership of stocks and positions of authority in business and industry, they had a good deal of power themselves. For a third, they had the time and money to devote to reform, which men and women working sixty hours a week for meager wages did not. Finally, the well-to-do were paying most of the taxes, and it was their money that was going into the bank accounts of the corrupt city bosses and their allies. The wealthy felt that the crime, disease, and general disorder of the slums threatened them, too. The motives of the reformers—the Yankee businessmen and the immigrant leaders— then, were mixed, as is often the case in human life. They genuinely wanted to improve their cities, wanted to make life easier for slum dwellers, immigrants, and working people in general. But they had something personal to gain from reform, too.

Thus, while the working class—native and immigrant—supplied the votes for reform, and some politicians like Tim Sullivan were reformers as well as bosses, most of the leadership for reform came from an elite, mostly businessmen. For example, one historian has discovered that two-thirds of the members of organizations supporting government reform in Pittsburgh were from an elite drawn from 2 percent of Pittsburgh's families. Chambers of commerce were almost always in the front of drives for city manager or commission forms of government; and chambers of commerce were made up of business leaders.

So the reforms went through. To be sure, not all reforms passed, and not all of them worked as they were supposed to. Even today we have city officials who take bribes and there are inefficiencies in street repair and garbage collection; even today we have pockets of poverty where crime and disease remain problems. But there is also no question that American cities today are far better places to live in than they were a hundred years ago.

The American city has, of course, changed. Today our cities, big and small, are surrounded by massive suburban belts that only barely existed

America has few national newspapers. Most papers are associated with cities, and are edited for the people who live in and around them, carrying news of local politics, home sporting teams, local amusements, as well as national news.

(left) Cities are the primary home for cultural events, like art exhibitions, theatrical performances, concerts. Here a jazz band performs in a city concert hall.

(right) New York's famous Lincoln Center, which combines several halls for the performance of opera, ballet, symphonies, and many other types of music, can really only exist in a city, where large numbers of people can be easily gathered together.

in the early 1900s. No longer does the majority of Americans live in central cities; life for these suburbanites is different from city life.

Nonetheless, the central cities are the focus of the suburbs. The city still is the heart of the nation, the place where we work and play. Without the cities they surround, the suburbs could not exist. The city still dominates America.

BIBLIOGRAPHY

For Teachers:

Addams, Jane. *Twenty Years at Hull House*. Edited with an Introduction by Victoria Bissell Brown. New York: St. Martin's Bedford Books, 1999.

Baldwin, Neil. *Edison, Inventing the Century*. New York: Hyperion, 1999.

Chudacoff, Howard P. and Judith Smith. *The Evolution of American Urban Society*. 5th ed. Englewood Cliffs: Prentice Hall, 1999.

Garfield, David R. and Blaine A. Brownell, *Urban America*. 2nd ed. Boston: Houghton Mifflin, 1990.

Grosvenor, Edwin S. Alexander Graham Bell: *The Life and Times of the Man Who Invented the Telephone*. New York: Harry N. Abrams, 1997.

Mackay, James A. *Sounds Out of Silence: A Life of Alexander Graham Bell*. Edinburgh, Mainstream Press, 1997.

Moll, Raymond A., ed. *The Making of Urban American*. Wilmington, DE: Scholarly Resources, 1997.

Monkkonen, Eric. *America Becomes Urban, 1780-1980*. Berkeley, University of California, 1998.

Riis, Jacob A. *How the Other Half Lives. Studies Among the Tenements of New York*. Edited with an Introduction by David Leviatin. New York: St. Martin's Bedford Books, 1996.

Shumsky, Neil Larry, ed. *Encyclopedia of Urban America*. 2 vols Santa Barbara, CA: ABC-CLIO, 1998.

Steffens, Lincoln. *The Shame of the Cities*. Introduction by Louis Joughin. New York: Hill and Wang, 1957.

Warner, Sam Bass. *The Urban Wilderness, A History of the American City*. Forward by Charles Tilly. Berkeley: University of California, 1995.

http://www.census.gov/population/www/documentation/twp50027.html (Largest hundred U.S. Cities, 1790-1990)

For Students:

Adair, Gene. *Thomas Alva Edison: Inventing the Electric Age*. New York: Oxford, 1996. (7+)

Hovde, Jane. *Jane Addams*. New York: Facts on File, 1989. (7+)

Leuzzi, Linda. *Urban Life.* New York: Chelsea House, 1995. (4 – 9)

Levinson, Nancy Smiler. *Turn of the Century: Our Nation a Hundred Years Ago.* New York: Lodestar/Dutton, 1994.

McPherson, Stephanie Sammartino. *Peace and Bread: The Story of Jane Addams.* Minneapolis: Carolrhoda, 1993.

Parker, Steve. *Thomas Edison and Electricity.* New York: Chelsea House, 1995.

Pasachoft, Naomi. *Alexander Graham Bell: Making Connections.* New York: Oxford, 1996. (7+)

Quiri, Patricia Ryon. *Alexander Graham Bell.* New York: Franklin Watts, 1991.

Sherrow, Victoria. *The Triangle Factory Fire.* Brookfield, CT: Millbrook Press, 1995.

Wright, David K. *A Multicultural Portrait of Life in the Cities.* Tarrytown, NY: Marshall Cavendish, 1994

Yepsen, Roger B. *City Trains: Moving Through America's Cities by Rail.* New York: Macmillan, 1993.

Page numbers for illustration are in **boldface**

Germans, 37–38, 67

government
city, 59, 60, 62, 63–65, 76–78, 79–80
federal, 77, 78
state, 74–75, 78–79

Great Lakes, 30

Greenwich Village, 46, **57**

gun control, 82

health, 54–55, 58, 72, 81

Hine, Lewis, **66**

Hone, Philip, 54

housing, 12–13, 16, 46, 56–57, 59–60.
See also building codes; buildings

Hull House, 81

hurricane, 78–79, **79**

immigrants, 35–38, **38**, 56–57, 61,
65–68, **66**

imports, 11–12

Independence Hall, 12

industrial revolution, 15–16, 25–27

initiative and referendum, 77–78

inns, 12

inventions, 25–27, 32, 34–35, 39–47,
46, 47

Irish, 37–38, 67

Italians, 65–66, **66,** 67

Japan, **24**

Jefferson, Thomas, 16

Jenney, William Le Baron, 47

Jews, 66–67

jobs, 35, 72
for city, 69–70, 77

journalists, 73. *See also* photographers

Kansas City, 80

kickbacks, 70, 72

laissez faire, 62

land, 70

language, 67

leisure, 51, 84

Lexington, 19

libraries, 14, 49

lightbulbs, 42

livestock, 54, **56**

Los Angeles, 44, 49, 78

Lowell, Francis Cabot, 17

Lowell, MA, 17–18

machines, 15, 25–27, 40, 43

manufactured goods, 15, 18

Maryland, 37

mayors, 76–77

medical centers, 9

metropolitan areas, 9

middle class, 71, 73, 76, 81

mills, 40, **40**

mill towns, 16, **17**

Milwaukee, 31, 37, 77

morals, 16, 17–18

Morgan, J. P., 76

Morse code, 34–35

moving pictures, 41

muckrakers, 73–74, **74**

museums, 49–50

music. *See* concert halls

JAMES LINCOLN COLLIER is the author of a number of books both for adults and for young people, including the social history *The Rise of Selfishness in America*. He is also noted for his biographies and historical studies in the field of jazz. Together with his brother, Christopher Collier, he has written a series of award-winning historical novels for children widely used in schools, including the Newbery Honor classic, *My Brother Sam Is Dead*. A graduate of Hamilton College, he lives with his wife in New York City.

CHRISTOPHER COLLIER grew up in Fairfield County, Connecticut and attended public schools there. He graduated from Clark University in Worcester, Massachusetts and earned M.A. and Ph.D. degrees at Columbia University in New York City. After service in the Army and teaching in secondary schools for several years, Mr. Collier began teaching college in 1961. He is now Professor of History at the University of Connecticut and Connecticut State Historian. Mr. Collier has published many scholarly and popular books and articles about Connecticut and American history. With his brother, James, he is the author of nine historical novels for young adults, the best known of which is *My Brother Sam Is Dead*. He lives with his wife Bonnie, a librarian, in Orange, Connecticut.

Fluvanna County High School
37[ ] Central Plains R[ ]
P[ ]ra, VA 22963